WOLF

RETURN TO YELLOWSTONE

MICHAEL MILSTEIN

THE BILLINGS GAZETTE · THE SOURCE

Published by The Billings Gazette
Wayne Schile, Publisher
Richard J. Wesnick, Editor

© 1995 The Billings Gazette

Written by Michael Milstein, reporter, The Billings Gazette
Edited by Richard J. Wesnick, Tom Tollefson and Ed Kemmick
Designed by Joyce Mayer, Graphic Design
Illustration by John Potter

Library of Congress Catalog Card Number 95-075503.
ISBN 0-9627618-8-5

For extra copies of this book contact:
The Billings Gazette, P.O. Box 36300, Billings, MT 59107-6300.
In Billings, call 657-1200. Or call toll-free from outside Billings, 1-800-543-2707.

Printed in the U.S.A.

BILLINGS GAZETTE · THE SOURCE

Above: Wolves have inspired both hatred and admiration in their long but uneasy relationship with humans. ALAN & SANDY CAREY

Facing page: A young two-year-old wolf waits to be flown into Yellowstone Park. MICHAEL MILSTEIN

Title page: Gray wolves shipped to Yellowstone Park first howled in response to the calls of nearby coyotes. Both species rely on howls as a means of staking out their territory and warning competitors away. ALAN & SANDY CAREY

Front cover photograph by ALAN & SANDY CAREY

Back cover top photograph courtesy of THE MONTANA HISTORICAL SOCIETY, HELENA, MONTANA

Back cover bottom photograph by ALAN & SANDY CAREY

CONTENTS

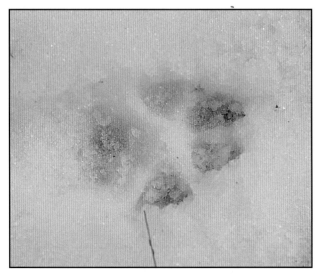

Above: Gray wolves excel at racing through deep snow. A wolf's anatomy allows it to conserve heat by routing blood away from its feet when they are in contact with snow.
ALAN & SANDY CAREY

Right: Tracks are only one of the characteristic calling cards that announce the presence of wolves as they roam their territories and hunt wild meals.
LURAY PARKER/WG&F/USFWS

INTRODUCTION

THE COMEBACK TRAIL

Blazing amid a still pillow of golden fur, the yellow eyes moved like dual compasses, tracking our every move as we tiptoed past. Sunlight was disappearing quickly. The last rays that slipped past the birch trees behind us cast a diamond around the piercing eyes, highlighting an already imposing stare.

"Even though no other muscle is moving, the eyes always are," said Steve Fritts, who was standing next to me.

For years, I had been writing about wolves and the fear and devotion that follow them, but never before had I seen a wild wolf. Fritts, a wildlife biologist with the U.S. Fish and Wildlife Service, had seen many wolves before, but his regard for the creature before us was no less than mine.

The keen eyes, seemingly the size of half dollars, belonged to a young male wolf lying on a bed of straw in a chain-link pen six feet wide, 12 feet long and six feet high. It looked odd among the heavy equipment, picnic tables and dry-docked buoys in the maintenance yard of a provincial park in western Alberta. The jagged peaks of Jasper National Park cut the horizon to the west. All around, highlands rolled and dipped like bunched-up carpet, carrying the Athabasca River toward the Canadian prairies to the east.

But the villain of children's fables, monster of horror movies and icon of the daunting wilderness before us would be going neither east nor west, where other wolves roam. Instead, it would be taken close to 750 miles south, to a point in the United States that, like the wolf, symbolizes wilderness. A place that, with the wolf back in place, may be the last, most complete portrait of untamed Nature in the Lower 48.

Yellowstone National Park.

Other wolves would later join this one on its journey to the world's first national park. Another bunch would go to the wilderness of central Idaho, a region so rugged it remains one of the largest tracts of forested land in the American West not sliced and diced by roads.

The caged young wolf we were looking at - two years old but as large as a German shepherd - was at the center of what is probably America's most celebrated, most condemned wildlife recovery project.

Irony is thick when it comes to wolves. For years near the turn of the century, taxpayers shelled out millions of dollars to get rid of wolves. Now, they are spending millions to bring them back. A government and a public that once poisoned wolves out of existence is now embracing the endangered species. Ranchers, seeing themselves as another kind of endangered species, fear wolves will drive their rustic ways out of existence. Wolves, the same lineage that gave rise to man's best friend, the domestic dog, were not so long ago man's worst enemy, a nagging pest.

Trapped, poisoned, shot, burned alive, ripped apart, wolves suffered as much persecution as humans could dish out. We did not know we missed them until they were gone.

The ragtag maintenance yard in Canada was deceptively calm. As the wolves shipped out on a cargo plane a few days later, soon to become the first of their kind beckoned back to the American West, they unknowingly assumed a daunting burden. Probably never before has a single band of a single species had so much riding on its shoulders.

Returning wolves will face scrutiny like never before: From biologists following the radio collars they wear. Ranchers fearing for their livestock. Environmentalists eager to restore balance to a world knocked out of kilter by the hand of man. Outdoorsmen convinced bureaucrats will use wolves as an excuse to close off public lands. Hunters worried that wolves will beat them to game. Travelers anxious to see loping wolves and hear their howl, a haunting voice that warns: You are not alone.

As Steve Fritts and I left the holding pens, a male black wolf leapt against the frame of its lockup behind us. Then he returned to anxious pacing. Every minute or so, the wolf would halt, look at us, and rattle the fence that caged him.

Perhaps it was some sense of the awaiting challenge that had the wolf on edge.

In late March 1995, wolves sprinted into Yellowstone Park's Lamar Valley for the first time in decades. With wolves back, the challenge is as much ours as it is theirs. We will decide whether we can resurrect wolves as effectively as we destroyed them.

When we killed wolves - hundreds of thousands of them - we never really gave ourselves a chance to know the creatures. Today, in Yellowstone National Park and the wilds of central Idaho, we finally have that chance.

Michael Milstein
The Billings Gazette

Rolling terrain, like the Hayden Valley, supports tens of thousands of elk, bison and other game, and leaves room for wolves to hunt and roam unmolested where visitors to Yellowstone might see them. LARRY MAYER

Above: In time, Americans began to believe their national parks should not be carefully managed scenes, but slices of unadulterated nature as they were before people took over.
ALAN & SANDY CAREY

ONE

HOWLS OF SILENCE

Breaking for a day from a military expedition in the summer of 1873, geologist Theodore Comstock set off to explore the heart of a green wilderness designated just a year before as America's first national park. Sloshing across Pelican Creek and winding through fallen timber, Comstock gawked at white towers of steam spiraling from hot springs atop a ridge overlooking the blue mirror of Yellowstone Lake. Among the springs, Comstock wrote in his journal, "none is more interesting than the Steamboat, the noise of which so closely resembles the puffing of a small lake-steamer that one involuntarily casts a longing eye over the surface of the water in the hope that such is really there."

Tangled tree trunks later slowed Comstock, so he stopped and made camp a few feet from a worn game trail, just below a small rise. He turned in early, but awoke when his mule, tethered nearby, struggled against its ties.

"I presently heard the doleful howl of a large wolf, which was slowly approaching along the trail," he wrote. He returned to sleep with his rifle beside him. In the morning, with mist cloaking the landscape, Comstock looked for traces of the wolf that had disturbed his slumber.

"A little investigation showed that the animal had been lying in the grass at the edge of the bluff, just above my head."

During the fitful night, Comstock became one of the first explorers to see and hear the reign-

ing predator of Yellowstone National Park. He was also one of the last.

In their struggle to both please people and preserve scenery, managers of the fledgling park created a portrait they thought travelers wanted to see. It reflected the promise of the American West: herds of game, towering peaks and thunderous cascades. But it also erased headstrong native peoples and unruly predators, chief among them the great gray wolf. A merciless campaign soon made the wolf as illusory as the steamer that Comstock had watched for off Steamboat Point.

Gone was one of the very elements that had made the West wild.

For thousands of years, the wolf had dominated the New World. We know because they left their remains.

More than 100 miles to the east of Yellowstone Park, on a limestone ridge jutting like a shelf from Wyoming's Bighorn Mountains, is a 15-foot cavity dark as the night sky. Looking down into the abyss, it's easy to tell how it came to be called Natural Trap Cave.

As prehistoric wolves trailed their quarry across a lush highland, both periodically took fatal plunges some 80 feet into the bell-shaped chamber. Dirt and dust sealed their remains until archaeologists descended on ropes and dug into the earthen diary. Layers from 10,000 to 20,000 years old yielded the bones of wolves. Also thousands of years ago, an ice age thawed and people found their way from Asia to North America across a now-submerged bridge of land. About the same time, prehistoric musk ox, buffalo, horses, camels and mastodons that had long dominated the continent disappeared.

For reasons not clear at the bottom of Natural Trap Cave, the gray wolf lived on. New prey - modern bison, moose and deer - appeared and the wolf flourished, spanning a worldwide range that once included all of the Lower 48 states. A shallow cave along Yellowstone Park's Lamar

Above: Wolf howls no longer resounded off Yellowstone's alpine peaks by the time early park rangers concluded their methodical destruction of the leading predators.
LARRY MAYER

River holds wolf bones more than 1,000 years old. Even then, wolves lived a kind of peaceful coexistence with human newcomers to the continent.

Those humans, our predecessors, left the traces Ken Cannon found by scratching dirt from a rectangular pit within spitting distance of Steamboat Point. As he worked, cars cruised by, some stopping so summer travelers could ogle the same hot springs Comstock had examined before his meeting with the wolf. Cannon, an unassuming National Park Service archaeologist, was looking for signs of earlier visitors to the terrain we know as Yellowstone.

What he uncovered atop the promontory were the remains of a bison, butchered 800 years ago by a Native American clan. Hearths and arrowheads at Steamboat and at ancient camp-grounds tell Cannon that people have traveled the land of the century-old park for close to 10,000 years. It's easy to assume such peoples were half-starved nomads who feared Yellowstone's spouting geysers - a tale spun to quell rumors of Indian attacks on park tourists. In reality, though, early peoples probably headed to Yellowstone for much the same reasons we do, to both revel in the warmth of the hot springs and find a wealth of game.

One difference: they saw wolves.

Wolves sit high in the spiritual hierarchy of many Indian tribes. Like wolves, Native Americans relied on cunning to make up what they lacked in speed and muscle. When hunting, when warring, tribes longed for the stealth,

Right: Wolves fell to the same westward expansion that wiped out millions of buffalo and drove Native Americans onto reservations. "This wolf had two traps on him, but when we approached him he set up and howled," a trapper wrote.
MONTANA HISTORICAL SOCIETY

Below: Early managers of Yellowstone Park tried to foster ever-larger herds of majestic elk and other big game by eliminating the carnivores that preyed on them. But the strategy backfired. BOB ZELLAR

stamina and acute senses of wolves. Warriors of the Nez Perce pushed wolf teeth between their nostrils. Blackfeet medicine men slept on wolf skins to absorb the wolf's strength and called the Milky Way, their heavenly path to the spirit world, the Wolf Trail. Pawnee scouts donned wolf pelts both as camouflage and transcendent links to the creatures that had worn them before.

But respect did not stop natives from killing wolves when they needed pelts, teeth or meat. Obsidian skinning tools unearthed in Yellowstone bear traces of canine blood. Carnivore livers are rich in minerals, so people may have sought them as a rudimentary vitamin supplement. Where Indians herded buffalo over cliffs to their deaths, archaeologists have found skeletons of wolves with their skulls bashed in. Per-

haps the natives were defending their spoils. But wolves chase prey off precipices, too. Perhaps they were not the ones appropriating the kill.

As modern times approached, it was the wolf's taste for cattle and sheep that made it an outlaw, first in the East, where livestock arrived from the Old World almost four centuries ago, and later in the West, ahead of a human tide lured by land and gold.

Masses of bison that darkened the plains fell to a tremendous assault for their hides, tongues, meat, or, sometimes, just to make room for progress. Hunters killed 50 million or more. Wolves - so dependent on the giant herds for food that western explorer Meriwether Lewis had called them "the shepherd of the buffalo" - stuffed themselves on the carcasses; as buffalo

*Yellowstone Lake appears
as a huge, blue mirror, much as
geologist Theodore Comstock
would have seen it during the
summer of 1873. The Teton
Range looms in the distance.*
LARRY MAYER

hunters sliced hides from their kills, wolves stood in the background, licking their chops. Their ranks swelled.

But soon they, too, fell under attack, at first for their furs, a ready substitute for the pelts of beaver already decimated by the fur trade. Wolf hunters, called "wolfers," laced bison remains with poison to liquidate wolves in droves. One traveler told of a Kansas settlement where about 75 yards of a road "had been artistically and scientifically paved with gray wolf carcasses." Many wolf skins went to adorn uniforms of the Russian army in what may have been a modern version of Native American lore. A novice wolfer who practiced for a week near Billings, Montana, tallied nine wolves and 26 coyotes. "Total profit," he boasted, "$118.50 and lots of fun."

Above: Plentiful game and few people gave early trappers the freedom to take as much wildlife as they wanted. Their lustrous fur put gray wolves near the top of the list. MONTANA HISTORICAL SOCIETY

Right: The same park rangers who presided over striking sights such as the Lower Falls of the Yellowstone killed Yellowstone's last wolves nearby. LARRY MAYER

Strychnine as a poison acted quickly. Photographs show poisoned wolves in a frozen tableau, a last supper of the wild; dead wolves sitting on their haunches, not even a look of surprise in their eyes.

Inflated wolf populations sealed their fate by turning from vanishing bison to the next best thing: cattle and sheep. Not only was such stock plentiful, but unlike fleet elk and deer and fortified bison, they also had no natural means to outwit wolves. Wolves were, rancher and President Theodore Roosevelt proclaimed, a "scourge to

Above: Gray wolves are very social animals that thrive on contact with each other. Dominant wolves sometimes skirmish with low-ranking animals to enforce their control over the pack. A lowered tail is a sign of submission. ALAN & SANDY CAREY

the stockmen" - mangling a half-million domestic animals, worth millions of dollars, each year.

By the 1870s, cash bounties hung over the wolf's head. In Oregon, alliances built for wolf control formed the foundation of state government. An unwritten law of the range called for cowboys to add pasty strychnine to any carcass they passed. Pushing the government to pay for extermination of wolves, like so many cockroaches, Sen. Thomas B. Kendrick of Wyoming told a Senate panel, "There is nothing so vicious in its cruelty as the method employed by the gray wolf in destroying his prey.

"His prey is literally eaten alive, its bowels torn out while it is still on its feet in many cases."

If there was an even more diabolical way to kill, though, Westerners probably tried it on wolves. There were steel traps that clamped shut on a wolf's foot. Pits lined with sharpened stakes. Knives embedded in frozen tallow that would cut the tongues of hungry wolves so they bled to death. Snares that strangled them. Broken glass spread on fresh meat. Fishhooks suspended be-

Right: Rather than snapshots, early visitors, including Civil War General William T. Sherman, took potshots at almost any wildlife they saw. When Sherman's party came across grizzly bears, their first concern was to shoot them. Bob Zellar

tween trees that would leave wolves hanging by their throats. Eskimos passed on an unerring technique: coil slender lengths of whalebone like a spring and fix them in blubber. Eaten by a wolf, the bone will unfurl like a flag in the wind and puncture the animal's insides. There was the method of tying female wolves on the range, waiting for males to arrive and then clubbing the suitors to death in the throes of their union. Smashing their jaws or wiring them shut so they would starve. Dousing wolves in gasoline and burning them alive. Cutting their hamstrings and siccing dogs on them. Roping and then dragging them behind horses.

Montana lawmakers seized upon mange, an affliction in which mites burrow beneath the skin, causing an animal's hair to fall out, after which it dies from exposure. In 1905, the Legislature ordered the state veterinarian to infect wolves with mange and release them in hopes of spreading the parasite. It is still spreading: the legislated outbreak may have given mange its first real foothold among Western wildlife.

Congress, starting in 1914, approved money to destroy wolves. Idaho leaders ordered state game wardens to "attain extermination of wolves, coyotes, wildcats and cougars." From 1919 to 1928, Idaho's wildlife agency poisoned, trapped or killed at least 258 wolves. Between 1883 and 1918, Montana paid $342,764 in bounties on 80,730 wolves. That may not be an entirely accurate figure, though. Wolfers frequently claimed cash for the same pelts in different states and claimed wolf bounties on badger or coyote skins when local officials couldn't tell the difference. Others killed pups, but left the parents to breed again, thereby ensuring themselves an income the following year.

A U.S. government "wolf control specialist" figured far more than $100 million in bounties went to wolfers during settlement of the West. The money finally pushed wolves over the brink.

National parks offered sanctuary to survivors of many species muscled from their ancestral homes by westward expansion. But they extended no clemency to wolves.

Standing above Tower Falls in Yellowstone Park, you see mist hovering about volcanic formations shaped like a child's sand castles. Cameras click, locking in the view. Beyond the falls lies the rust-striped canyon of the Yellowstone River. About 30 miles upstream, a day's travel for a wolf, is Yellowstone Lake and Steamboat Point. Across the canyon, Specimen

Left: Death is part of the natural cycle in Yellowstone, whether a wolf, disease, harsh weather or starvation brings it on.
LARRY MAYER

Moose and other large game grazed peacefully in Yellowstone after wolves fell to a merciless assault. BOB ZELLAR

Ridge, sprinkled with hunks of petrified wood, stands above the pines.

It is roughly here that the wolves of Yellowstone made their last stand.

When President Ulysses S. Grant signed the bill establishing Yellowstone National Park in 1872, no one was quite sure what to make of the place. There had never been a national park before. At the time, the same tender view of the West that led people to think there were enough buffalo to last forever probably made them think the same of the wilderness and wildlife surrounded by Yellowstone's boundaries.

With plenty of wildness to go around, those who ran the park set about retooling Yellowstone to create what they thought was an attractive scene. A scene that did not include wolves.

Ledgers of early explorers like Comstock mention wolves now and then, but wolves were never as abundant as deer and elk, bison and bears. Any chance of seeing wildlife was iffy then, as it is now. A case study: Truman Everts, of the 1870 Washburn Expedition, the first organized foray into what is now Yellowstone Park. Everts spent 37 days wandering through forests and canyons after he got lost somewhere near Heart Lake, in Yellowstone's southern reaches. In an account of his ordeal, during which he lived off the roots of a plant (now called the Everts thistle) boiled in hot springs, Everts recalled hearing two long, deep wolf howls, a sound that made him "insensible to all other forms of suffering."

Legislation setting Yellowstone aside called for the Secretary of Interior to prevent "wanton destruction" of wildlife. But as foreign as the new national park itself was the notion of spending money on it. So Yellowstone wildlife initially had no more protection than its remote location could provide. Even that was not much.

Marauding market hunters had killed 7,000 elk since 1870, plus countless bighorn sheep, moose and bison, Superintendent Philetus W. Norris reported glumly in 1877. The image was no kinder than elsewhere in the West. Animals went not for food, "but mostly for their pelts and tongues, often run down on snowshoes and tomahawked when their carcasses were least valuable, and merely strychnine-poisoned for wolf or wolverine bait." Poaching, profiteering and spineless superintendents finally led the Secretary of Interior to dump Yellowstone in the hands of the U.S. Cavalry.

Scarce since the days of poisoning, wolves rallied, trailing elk from alpine pastures on the Mirror Plateau to wintering grounds along the Lamar River in 1915. Biologist Vernon Bailey "found big wolves common, feeding their young on elk, and probably also on buffaloes." But the old curse lingered. Wolves, a superintendent ruled, were "a decided menace to the herds of elk, deer, mountain sheep and antelope." A ranger finally got close enough to kill four skittish wolves along Slough Creek, opposite the north face of Specimen Ridge.

Two turns on Capitol Hill added politics to the mix. First, Congress backed predator control in the West, hinting at money for agencies that would stifle wolves. Second, Congress in 1916 created the National Park Service to run the ever-popular national parks. Since the new agency was eager for cash, it was eager to please. Lawmakers had ordered the Park Service to protect parks "unimpaired for the enjoyment of future generations," but also permitted destruction of "detri-

Above: Rangers hunting wolves in Yellowstone sometimes retrieved wolf pups and showed the cuddly youngsters to park visitors before killing them. YELLOWSTONE NATIONAL PARK

mental" animals. Yellowstone's rulers interpreted the edict loosely.

Predators might keep game under control, early Superintendent Robert Toll explained, but they would also cut the take of hunters, leaving the Park Service with "no support whatsoever from the sportsmen's associations of the adjoining states." He echoed the doctrine of his time: Yellowstone was meant to be manipulated by people, for people. Park rangers dumped garbage to attract bears to playful "lunch counters," while tourists watched from bleachers. They fed elk and buffalo. They loosed foreign fish into park waters, playing havoc with native species. They poured soap into geysers to coax eruptions. They boated to islands in Yellowstone Lake to stomp the eggs of pelicans that ate trout.

And from 1915 on, despite a few murmurs of protest, they slew wolves with a vengeance.

Below and to the east of Specimen Ridge, the Lamar River points toward the bristling peaks of the Beartooth Mountains. Off to the west is Hellroaring Creek, weaving through the rattling rapids that gave the stream its name. Wolves that once lived here seemed to know they were marked for death. For days, rangers watched a wolf den on a rocky slope above Hellroaring Creek, itching to shoot its occupants. Elk skulls, the remains of past meals, lay scattered about the entrance.

Finally, the adult wolves grew suspicious and toted their pups off. A few weeks later, rangers discovered the substitute den a mile away, tucked into jumbled slabs of rock. Eight feet in, amid hunks of fresh elk meat left by adult wolves, the rangers found seven pups about three weeks old and killed them all.

A big pack of 16 wolves crossed Specimen Ridge a few years later, but moved on. The body count continued: 1918, 36 wolves killed; February 1919, signs of wolves north of Specimen Ridge - "efforts are being made to exterminate them"; April 1920, 14 wolves killed, including 13 pups in two dens near Tower Falls, pups buried alive in another den on Blacktail Creek; April 1921, adult male ("biggest ever") and 11 pups destroyed; May 1922, destroyed two adults and six pups on Specimen Ridge - "the work of controlling these animals must be vigorously prosecuted"; April 1923, female killed at den near Tower Falls, five pups sent to park headquarters for exhibition.

All told, at least 136 park wolves, more than half of them pups, died between 1914 and 1926. East of Specimen Ridge, rangers in 1926 trapped two pups near the old hot spring cone called Soda Butte. They were the last successors of the wolf that had lolled above Comstock's camp. Wolf tracks grew rare - 1924: "Signs of wolf exceedingly scarce," 1928: "There have been no wolf sign reported this season." A few skulls went into the attic of the Smithsonian Institution.

Nothing else was left.

Above: Epic forest fires that rampaged through Yellowstone Park in 1988 opened new meadows where elk now graze. BOB ZELLAR

Overleaf: The undulating Pitchstone Plateau testifies to the vastness of Yellowstone National Park. LARRY MAYER

HATRED AND HUMANITY

Cowboy hats bobbed atop the crowd inside the auditorium in Cody, Wyoming. Worn stripes outlined basketball courts on the wood-paneled floor, scarred by scuffs of competitions past. This first day of September saw a different kind of contest, one warranting a "no alcohol, no weapons, no signs, no animals" warning on the door. Those waiting for their three minutes behind a microphone at the front of the room, and the hundred or so listening, were players in a moral struggle of sorts - one that could shape the future of people and wildlife in the West.

Yellow leaves on the trees outside filtered the sun, a reminder the last days of the 1993 summer were near. In the highlands to the west, along the east flank of the craggy peaks that fall away from Yellowstone National Park's high plateau, deer, elk and moose were rapidly learning this was the opening day of hunting season.

Which was appropriate, since those inside the gym were debating the reinstatement of perhaps the most clever and cutthroat hunter around.

The first behind the microphone was local County Commissioner Jack Winninger. He told how his father, new to the sheep business in Wyoming at the turn of the century, had spent much of his life trying to stamp out this relentless killer.

Left: Wolves faced persecution in the early West because their superior hunting skills made their species one of the few that competed directly with a river of human settlers. ALAN & SANDY CAREY

Above: Without wolves, elk herds in Yellowstone swelled so much they began wearing the range thin, leaving them vulnerable to starvation during difficult winters. BOB ZELLAR

Right: By limiting the size of big game herds, wolves tended to keep the herds in line with the capacity of their grazing lands. ALAN & SANDY CAREY

"To me as a little boy," he said soberly, "I can remember the big bad wolf is a lot worse than the three bears."

Set a map of Yellowstone National Park on a dining room table. Find Cody and then give the map a one-quarter turn. Bozeman, Montana, will appear in its place. There, a similar meeting filled a room at the turn-of-the-century Baxter Hotel. Jack Gladstone spoke first, giving the views of the Blackfeet Indian Nation.

"Time did not begin with Christopher Columbus 500 years ago," he told the assembly. "It has only been about 100 years since this massive warfare between the wolves and the Western civilization has occurred. And what we are looking at now in this Yellowstone National Park area is to see one area here returned to its former balance and glory."

Such was the battle over the wolf, a political push and pull that during the late summer of 1993 brought a species efficiently eliminated by a government not noted for its efficiency closer than ever to a renaissance. It was impossible not to recall the days of Winninger's father, when the nation blamed wolves for hobbling Western progress. I tried to envision such old-timers standing around the basketball floor in Cody, to see the expression on their crinkled faces. Since their time, the vision of the West had changed. A dozen decades since geologist Theodore Comstock had faced a wolf in a very young Yellow-stone National Park and decades since that

animal's descendants had perished, wolves themselves had become - for many - an icon of progress in humanity's respect for the natural world.

Wolves, the nation would finally decide, are as much a part of Yellowstone as lions are a part of the Serengeti.

Along about the time wolf friends and foes gathered in towns that surround Yellowstone Park and central Idaho, the fall's first snow dusted western Alberta. An ebony female wolf topped a ridge, leaving four-toed tracks in the fresh Canadian powder. Her pack followed, sniffing for prey to help them through the coming winter.

This was her home territory, the only country she had ever known. But it would not be the last.

For the same plodding, bureaucratic machine that prompted the late-summer meetings would eventually draft the big female (close to 100 pounds) as a pioneer. Little more than a year later, she would lead her kind to a land from which they had been ruthlessly evicted.

Consider a time-line on the wall. Start it at 1872, the birth date of Yellowstone Park. End it at the present. It will show that people took about as long to bring wolves back as to eradicate them in the first place.

No more gunshots rang across Yellowstone's Hellroaring Creek, Specimen Ridge or anyplace else wolves had set up house when the National Park Service in 1933 decreed that it would protect, not destroy, such predators as the wolf. No sudden revelation had stifled the carbines. Rather, the silence responded to an equally mute terrain, absent the howls that had reverberated before. No wolves were left to kill.

For a time, the campaign to rid the West of its carnivores looked like a success. Ranchers flourished, grazing their longhorns on cheap public range. The hunting of coyotes and other leftover predators (including grizzly bears that scrapped with tourists) continued in national parks before the new predator-friendly edict filtered through the ranks. Not to worry: people flocked to Yellowstone, seduced by hay-fed elk and bison that flowed along river bottoms like streams of fur. During the first decade of National Park Service rule in Yellowstone, visitation quadrupled to nearly 200,000 (still fewer than a tenth of today's numbers).

It was not long before cracks shot through the facade.

For starters, the wildlife that tourists adored, including bighorn sheep, pronghorn antelope and deer, were disappearing even as rangers sought to protect them by killing coyotes.

Facing public fury for both the vanishing game and the killing of carnivores, park managers granted coyotes a reprieve and, in 1937, called in Adolph Murie, a young biologist, to solve the puzzle. He spent two years gathering coyote droppings - 5,086, to be precise. After wrapping them in paper or cheesecloth (the deposits "vary considerably in size and conformation," he explained) Murie picked the droppings apart, looking for bones, fur or leaves - exacting clues about the dining habits of the animals that had left them.

Left: As federal agencies tested the national attitude toward wolves, they found public support for bringing wolves back to Yellowstone's mountains and valleys outweighed the opposition. LARRY MAYER

Above: As biologists came to understand nature's interlocking framework, they realized that large vegetarians such as buffalo are not the only important wildlife. Steely jawed predators are, too. LARRY MAYER

His findings shook the customary view that antlered vegetarians - bighorn sheep, elk, bison, deer and so on - wear the white hats of the animal kingdom while toothy meat-eaters that devour them don black. Yellowstone's problem was not too many predators, Murie concluded, but too few: with the assault on the wolf, mountain lion (121 killed in the previous three decades) and coyote (4,352 killed), plus the feeding of big game already protected from hunting, elk herds were multiplying out of control, trampling the land to dust and leaving little for anyone else. Ranches and tourist developments by then had much of the park surrounded, co-opting lowlands where game had long wintered.

Racing to set things right, Yellowstone's handlers did just the opposite. Rangers gunned down thousands of elk. The herds responded by multiplying even faster. Rangers corralled elk and bison and sent them to zoos. No luck. In short, they did everything to curb the hordes except recall the one master hunter that had culled them for ages.

But Yellowstone's decades of damage control did foster the first half of a providential trade.

Of the excess elk removed from the park, hundreds were shipped north to Alberta, where overhunting had abolished their kind. This territory, hugging the Canadian Rockies, also harbored wolves, forebears of a certain female that would trek through snowdrifts years later. A wolf that, in a kind of ultimate tit-for-tat between hunter and hunted, would appear in Yellowstone to stalk the same line of elk that once fortified her ancestors.

After Yellowstone, Adolph Murie turned his attention to wolves prowling Alaska's Mount McKinley National Park, known now as Denali. They had been persecuted as wolves had in Yellowstone. After three seasons of traipsing across a land of glaciers and crumbling crags, gathering 1,174 wolf droppings and inspecting 821 skulls and other shreds of Dall sheep, many killed by wolves, Murie found striking parallels with his former turf. On verdant grasslands where lambs were well-fed and strong, "there was little predation," Murie wrote in 1941. But when mule deer in Yellowstone, or sheep in Mount McKinley, nibbled on range already frayed like a worn suit, fawns withered through the winter until coyotes killed them. Death is never pretty. But Murie learned that coyotes and wolves deal it out with consummate skill, balancing the size of game herds with the capacity of the range they browse.

Our distaste for the bloody way predators do business had blinded us to their purpose, as if we had shunned butcher shops because butchers slice up red meat.

Where Murie left off, Aldo Leopold picked up. Protecting only favored species, like deer and elk, said the father of modern wildlife management, was no better than preserving only a few colorful threads from an ancient tapestry and expecting it to last.

Leopold came to rue the day he and a fellow forester had pumped bullets into a family of wolves that romped into the open while they ate lunch. They reached the old female as her fierce green eyes winked out. Leopold may have remembered those eyes when, in 1944, he asked why wolves could not endure in Yellowstone Park and its surrounding national forests "Why," he wondered, "in the necessary process of extirpating wolves from the livestock ranges of Wyoming and Montana, were not some of the uninjured animals used to restock the Yellowstone?"

This query from a leader of the conservation movement did not stop the government from ridding the nation of wolves. Close to 50 years later, though, America would face up to the question.

And its answer would resound 1,000 miles north, into Alberta, where a big, black female wolf ambled, stopping to raise her nose for prey and again to howl out advice to others, across forested bottomlands of the McLeod River. This wolf, like Leopold's, pierced the shadowy timber with eyes that reflected a fierce green.

These eyes, however, were very much alive.

Two bends in American wildlife policy revived Leopold's question. First, his son A. Starker Leopold chaired a blue-ribbon panel that decreed in 1963 that national parks should portray a slice of "primitive America." Then, a decade later, Congress passed the Endangered Species Act, ordering government biologists to protect and restore species absent from their original range.

Including the wolf. It was quite an about-face for a country that had once legislated the wolf into oblivion.

The first 14 gray wolves brought to Yellowstone were kept in three one-acre pens in the Lamar Valley as part of a federal program to reintroduce the predators to their former haunts in Yellowstone National Park. Trapped in Canada and shipped to the park in January, 1995, all of the wolves were released from their pens in March, 1995.

Mammoth

Tower

Norris

Lamar Valley

Canyon Village

West Thumb

Fishing Bridge

Yellowstone Lake

N

Yellowstone National Park

Gray Wolf — Canis Lupus ("Wolf Dog")

Largest of the wild canines, adult males can average 95 to 125 pounds and females about 15 pounds less. A large wolf may stretch 7 feet from nose to tip of tail and stand 3 feet high at the shoulder.

A gray wolf's pelage ranges from pure white to coal black, with a wide variety of grays and browns in between.

Wolf Track
(Actual Size)

Right: As proposals to bring wolves back to Yellowstone Park surfaced again and again, local residents feared incoming carnivores would decimate the grand palette of wildlife in the region.
LARRY MAYER

Below: Many people came to view wolves not as a pest to be exterminated, but as a missing component of wilderness.
ALAN AND SANDY CAREY

Yellowstone's hot springs and geysers prompted the park's creation, but today Yellowstone is also known for its rich array of wildlife.
LARRY MAYER

What followed was two decades of politics - plans drawn up, cast aside, revised, turned over to committees, studied, dropped, revived, handed to new committees.

A pair of hangups dragged it out. Number one: bureaucracy. Number two: all the same reasons that people had wanted to get rid of the wolf to begin with.

Locals did not want to play second fiddle to a fiend of horror movies, especially with the government producing the show. Polls showed that more than 80 percent of visitors to Yellowstone wanted wolves back in the park, but intense lo-

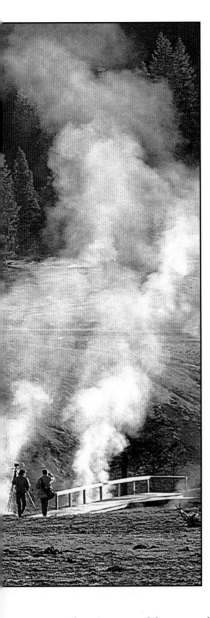

cal resistance, like a small but determined brigade holding off attackers, outdid the will of the majority for years.

"You ought to be dad-gum happy it's not a vote," Ed Bangs of the U.S. Fish and Wildlife Service told 150 people packed into the high school gymnasium in Meeteetse, Wyoming, one warm July evening in 1992. Meeteetse is a true cowtown. Its sidewalks are real wood, abraded by cowboy boots. Down the road, near Cody, a hand-painted sign advises: "Wyoming is cow country. Enjoy beef." It's signed, "Meeteetse Cowbelles." Whoever the Cowbelles are, they

surely have an opinion about wolves. Probably the same opinion as the people in the crowded gymnasium, eyeing Bangs like a cow at a Meeteetse barbecue.

Ed Bangs may be about the only federal wildlife biologist who could get away with saying "dad-gum" to a roomful of cowboys. He's tall and lanky and looks like he ought to be gnawing a stem of wheatgrass. He has worked with wolves in Alaska. When Congress decided in 1991 it was high time for an environmental impact statement to seriously examine bringing wolves back to the American West, Bangs got the assignment. Part of the job was to take his show on the road and explain to people who raise livestock that might be attacked by wolves and who are suspicious of just about anything the government does and who would rather the feds just kept their noses out of things, thank you, especially since they burned that Yellowstone Park down, that wolves aren't so bad, after all.

Which wasn't really what the crowd in Meeteetse wanted to hear, since someone asked all those who did not want wolves to raise their hands and everyone did.

(Meeteetse folks had experience with endangered species; back in 1981, the only remaining colony of black-footed ferrets was discovered nearby after a rancher's dog caught one.)

Bangs plunged ahead with his slide show, sprinkled with "Far Side" cartoons. He allowed as how it's easy to be for wolves when it's not your livestock that will get chewed and said he understood why locals see wolves as a sign of big government, as another spotted owl. But wolves just do not live up to their imagined depravity. Most people like them.

"We get boxes of mail every day from people who want wolves back," he said.

After Bangs (the event had been billed as a debate, but Bangs wouldn't debate) came Troy Mader, a clean-cut young man who drove a station wagon with a "NO WOLVES" bumper sticker bearing a wolf with a red line through it. He represented the Abundant Wildlife Society of North America, an outfit in Gillette, Wyoming, that did not want wildlife so abundant as to include wolves.

He showed slides of wolf-shredded livestock and game and said that is what people will see if wolves come back. Actually, people might not see even that, he guessed, because people might avoid the national park so as not to be maimed by rabid wolves.

There was a slide of a bull moose, its antlers wide as a grown man. "You can see a moose like this," Mader said.

Next on the screen was a bloody carcass. "Or this."

Like the faceoff in the Meeteetse gymnasium, the wider debate was going nowhere. Perhaps the only ones that could jar the multimillion-dollar wolf recovery machine forward were the wolves themselves.

And so they did.

In August of that same summer, a wildlife filmmaker shooting footage of grizzly bears in Yellowstone Park's Hayden Valley filmed something else feeding on the carcass of a buffalo: a black canine that was not a coyote. Lone wolves were already roaming national forests in Idaho.

On the last day of September, hunter Jerry Kysar leapt off his horse just south of Yellowstone Park and fired his rifle at the biggest of four or five coyotes scattering like snowflakes through burned timber. The one he killed was not a coyote, which are hunted freely in Wyoming.

It was a wolf, related to packs that had meandered from Canada into northern Montana's

Glacier National Park - too far from Yellowstone, biologists thought, for an entire pack to go.

Reports of wolves in and around Yellowstone had filtered in before, including a bunch about 1970 when rumors flew about a secret wolf transplant. But no solid evidence. Suddenly, here was a wolf that had trekked 300 miles or more, topped the Continental Divide, negotiated four-lane interstates and arrived in Yellowstone, where no wolves were supposed to be.

"It was like shooting a dinosaur," Kysar said.

You could almost hear them say it: Ready or not, here we come.

The next two years, in brief: 160,000 public comments received, many the result of intense lobbying by environmental groups. There were more comments than any other federal action had drawn. People wanted wolves.

Somewhere in the forests of Alberta, a green-eyed female awaited a rendezvous with Yellowstone.

Above: A wolf's body language often reveals its mood. Raised tail and bared teeth may signal both dominance and aggression, while lowered tails and teeth hidden behind jowls show submission to higher-ranking animals.
ALAN AND SANDY CAREY

If any one place in the Lower 48 could accommodate every component of the natural world, including gray wolves, Yellowstone Park and the mass of surrounding national forests was probably the place. LARRY MAYER

The gray fur of some wolves blends into the snowy landscape where they roam. While human eyes sometimes reflect red in the light, wolf eyes, and those of many other predators, reflect green. LuRay Parker/Wyoming Game & Fish

THREE

A FAMILY OF VALUES

Sun flares off thick snow weighing down the prairie grass. I wait for my eyes to adjust after roaring out of shady timber aboard a big, boxy Ski-doo, a vintage snowmobile on loan from Alberta's fish and wildlife agency. Gerald Gustavson rides ahead of me and, having trapped along the Canadian Rockies for more than a decade, is plenty used to this. He is up, off his Ski-doo (Canadian parlance for snowmobile, no matter what its make), studying the brilliant snow. He takes only a few seconds to declare his find.

"This is what we're after," Gerry says.

Looking toward his feet, I know exactly what he's talking about. A big footprint, as wide as my size 12 boot. I yank my mitten off, bend down and find my palm will not cover the track. Four toes. Broad heel. Damn big.

Wolf.

As striking as the raw size of the print is its timing. Gerry and I had passed this way the same morning, about two hours before. Here is this whopping footprint, atop OUR trail.

"They pay attention to what we're up to," Gerry says, with more than a hint of admiration.

Seeing the track is a bit disconcerting, in an exhilarating sort of way, like speeding down a hill on a bicycle a little faster than your mother would want. Something else is out there, this track shouts, something much smarter in the ways of the wild. It's hard not to think for a

moment about all the fanciful, outrageous tales: Little Red Riding Hood, werewolf hysteria that rivaled the Salem witch trials, and even Theodore Roosevelt, to whom the wolf was "a beast of waste and desolation."

But as you begin to know wolves as Gerry knows wolves, as you soak up the lessons wolves have taught him and as you sip his spiced rum (very tasty), any trepidation about the creatures matures into respect, even awe. They reward and promote, within their close-knit families, the same talents and strengths we do. You begin to wonder just how different we are from the beast who left the track that outsizes my hand.

Gerry is roaming the bush in early December 1994 because he's one of about a dozen Canadian trappers the U.S. government has hired to get a handle on wolf populations in western Alberta. An environmental impact statement in mid-1994 had ended an American tug-of-war

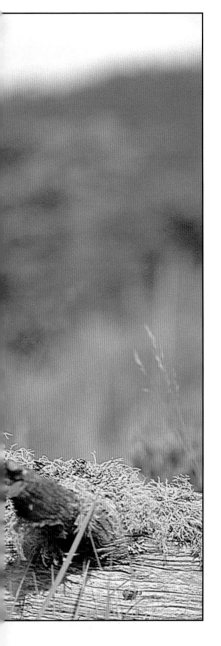

Above: Canadian trapper Gerald Gustavson cannot always catch wolves, but he can usually find their tracks. MICHAEL MILSTEIN

Pups practice their hunting skills on insects and mice near their den, but by the time they are a year old, they cooperate with the rest of their pack to go after bigger prey. ALAN & SANDY CAREY

and cleared a path for wolves to return, with a helping hand, to Yellowstone Park and central Idaho. A purchase order tacked in Gerry's cabin lists the transaction: "Provide wolves for Yellowstone reintroduction." Biologists will fit captured wolves with radio collars and turn them loose, paying trappers $2,000 per animal. When U.S. agencies begin searching out packs for Yellowstone and Idaho, the collared "Judas wolves" will betray the hideouts of their packs.

True, some wolves had already arrived in Yellowstone and Idaho. One left footprints in the park in mid-1993; several others were tooling through Idaho. It's possible, even likely, that wolves surging south from Canada into northwest Montana, around Glacier National Park, would reclaim the ground without our help. But given the distances and sheer bulk of wildlands (more than 11 million acres, twice the size of Maryland) in and around Yellowstone and the

potential for lone wolves to wander and wander without ever finding a friend, biologists thought it could take decades for wolves to pair up and form packs.

And that was just too long to wait.

There's also a legalistic reason. Wolves on their own are an endangered species. Shooting them risks a fine and prison time. If the feds import them, however, the wolves would be an "experimental population," and more accountable. If experimental wolves start tearing up cattle, ranchers can do something about it.

Experimental is not a word that goes easily with the black female wolf that guides her pack, strung out in single file behind her, through mountain streams in Canada. Her eyes reflect a pale green moon. There is no question who is in charge.

She is clearly the "alpha" female of her pack. Packs hinge on an alpha male and female. They lead hunts and rub out rivals. Only they usually breed. Typical packs number five to 10 wolves, rounded out by pups and siblings a year older. Wolves normally leave their packs after two seasons, when they are old enough to breed. Outcasts sometimes trail packs, scavenging hungrily for leftovers. Subordinate wolves incessantly test their parents, ready to seize on any chance to pull a rapid-fire coup.

But the big, black female stands her ground.

When gray wolves hunt lumbering bison, they tend to test the herd, striking mainly at the weaker animals. That gives the stronger animals a better shot at survival.
LARRY MAYER

Late in the previous winter, she and her mate had paired up. About two months afterward, the family gave up their nomadic ramblings chasing prey and dug a den into a gentle hillside. Lying in the snug, black chamber, sounds of the forest outside muffled by earth, the matron gave birth to six pups, plus or minus a few. At first, they were just wriggling fur balls. Within another month, their eyes had opened and they tumbled out of the den, sniffing and snuffling the new world.

Like the fond aunts and uncles they were, others in the pack doted on the youngsters, refereeing tussles, even babysitting while the alphas led part of the pack on nighttime hunts. When the hunters returned to the den or other preset rendezvous points, amid anxious licking and tail wagging, they disgorged meat that the pups eagerly gobbled. As the pups matured through the summer, the pack again roved its territory. Older siblings gallivanted alone like teenagers with wanderlust. The pups learned their trade, pouncing on grasshoppers and mice and filling out feet splayed like snowshoes.

The black alpha and a tawny female pup, cut in her image, covered much the same ground together.

Wolves remain in Alaska and the Upper Midwest states, but U.S. agencies wanted wolves from the Canadian Rockies because they are closer, genetically speaking, to animals that once prowled the American end of the mountain range. Those lost animals had once claimed their own subspecies, *Canis lupus irremotus,* which means: The wolf who is always showing up. When they stopped showing up, their narrow skulls and gray color scheme vanished, too. Since then, specialists have plugged dimensions of hundreds of wolf skulls into computers and found too little difference to warrant many subspecies.

They now figure the northern Rocky Mountain wolf that called Yellowstone and Idaho home was one race, more or less, of *Canis lupus,* the gray wolf.

Which is what left the tracks Gerry and I are looking at in the middle of his trapline. A trapline is not, as I had assumed, a line of traps waiting to snap shut on an unsuspecting foot. Instead, it's a piece of government forest - "crown land" - where Gerry has paid for sole trapping rights. On the map, it's long and skinny, roughly two by 20 miles. On the ground, it's a busy place. Logging trucks whine down dirt lanes; a cow moose and its calf amble after tasty greens; oil exploration crews roll through the trees, drilling slots for explosives that should betray any black gold below; and we chug around on Ski-doos.

None of this fazes Gerry, who says, "That's our economy." It must not bother the wolves much either, because their tracks are all over the place.

As we cruise hardpacked alleys seismic crews have cut through the trees, we see the wolves have, too. They're not dumb, these animals. Wolves let moose and caribou serve as snowplows and follow their paths through deep powder, perhaps looking to turn the snowplow into a meal. A man working for the Hudson Bay Company in the Canadian North during the late 1800s saw wolves take trails blazed by sled dog teams: packs would stand atop knolls until the dog team got far enough ahead and then pace to the next knoll and wait again.

I slow the snowmobile and look over my shoulder. Nothing.

But just off the trail, below a leafless bush, is a yellow patch in the snow. To biologists, it's a wolf's "scent mark." To the wolf, like its cousin the dog, it's a signpost that, at a quick sniff, broadcasts the lay of the land.

As soon as the black alpha female and her tawny gray pup took up residence inside their one-acre pen in Yellowstone Park, they tugged at the wall, looking for a passage to freedom. Their faces were smeared with blood from elk carcasses provided by the biologists. YELLOWSTONE NATIONAL PARK

Wolves patrolling their territories leave scent-marks every few minutes, usually by urinating, but also by defecating. The sign not only notifies wolves whether they are in their own pack's territory or trespassing on another's, but given the wolf's sense of smell (100 times more sensitive than our own) it also offers other clues: how recently another wolf has passed through, whether a kill lies nearby or whether the presiding alpha pair have linked up. To make the most of their postings, leading wolves - particularly alpha males - lift a leg to leave their scent on a tree or bush up off the ground, making it all the more apparent to passers-by.

Such notices may carry a more distinct message. Sometimes when Gerry checks his snares - wire nooses hidden in the shade around baits of road-killed elk, deer or moose - he finds where a wolf has trotted up to one of the wire loops, sniffed it and relieved itself on the snare. Wolves will also, he says, "water the tires on my truck."

It's as if they are taunting the rotund trapper: Go ahead, dumb human being, try to come and get me.

"They know why I'm here and what I'm doing," Gerry says. "They're telling me exactly what they think of it."

Photo albums in Gerry's cabin show him and his sons with beaver pelts and marten furs. Five years passed before he caught his first wolf. Before setting snares, the trapper now boils them with lye and spruce needles to cook out any human scent. He knows many wolves are already wise to his ways; they learn and they never repeat a mistake. It balances out. Sometimes he wins, sometimes they win. He keeps them on their toes, he figures, so they don't rip into livestock. If wolves were vanishing from Canada as they have from so much of the United States, Gerry says, "I'd be fighting as hard as anyone to save them."

Naturalist Ernest Thompson Seton must not have felt that way. He set out in 1894 to stop "Lobo," a wily wolf that had terrorized the Currumpaw Valley of New Mexico, killing thousands of cattle. The wolf and its pearly white mate, Blanca, eluded hunters and dug up traps. When Seton scattered poison baits, Lobo gingerly collected them, stacked them up and left his droppings atop the pile. Concealing traps next to a cow carcass, Seton finally trapped Blanca and strangled her. Finding loyalty a weakness (wolves make devoted mates), Seton set 130 steel traps and dragged Blanca's carcass over them. A day later, he found Lobo spread-eagled, each foot straining in a trap. Seton chained the wolf and left him gazing at his former kingdom. The next morning, all on his own, Lobo was dead.

Before the old, 150- pound wolf died, Seton had heard him howling, vainly summoning the rest of his band.

Howling sends an immediate signal. There is no mistaking the sound - long, deep, broken toward the end - that echoes wildness to its very core.

Just as each person has a distinctive voice, every wolf has a howl. Varying howls tell foreign packs: Keep out of our territory or else. Like a football team in a huddle, they say: We're excited we're together. Or they tell wanderers from the same pack: We've found food, come and get it.

Gerry finds where wolves have killed, the story written in the snow. Here's where the moose was idling, chomping leaves. Here's where the wolves came calling. Picture them tensed in silent standoff. A pair rush and sink the biggest of their 42 teeth (nearly two inches long) into the moose's haunches, tearing at muscles. Wolves latch onto the loins, nearly jaw to jaw with each other. The moose wheels. Another wolf leaps, plunging fangs into the rubbery nose. Even when the moose lifts and rolls its head, the wolf holds tight to the snout, swinging through the air like an elephant's trunk.

It's hazardous duty. A kick from a half-ton moose cracks ribs and skulls. Half of 110 wolves examined in Alaska bore healed fractures or broken bones that may have slowed them, but did not stop them.

Battle scars like this make wolves judicious. They do not butcher every animal they happen across, not by a long shot. While studying wolves at Isle Royale National Park in Michigan, biologist L. David Mech saw wolf packs encounter 131 moose, but kill only six. Other moose either evaded or outran wolves, which sprint about 35

Right: Even when wolves come across attractive prey, they do not always attack. Often they wait until an animal is vulnerable - wandering on its own or stuck in deep snow. BOB ZELLAR

mph, or faced them down. Wolves never charged any of the 26 moose that stood up to them. Just fleeing must send a subtle message. Perhaps the wolves think: If this animal were strong, it wouldn't be running away. It must know something we don't. And so they follow.

(This might explain instances where wolves trot right through livestock to hunt wild prey. Cattle rarely run. As Gerry puts it: "The wolf is so flabbergasted, he says, 'Leave this thing alone.'")

Wolves will certainly rush a prime animal if they have a chance - say, if it's floundering in deep snow - but tend to pick off the easier marks: puny fawns, arthritic elk, pronghorn antelope not quite as fleet-footed as the rest, the ones that take more from the herd (by eating communal grass or spreading illness) than they give back through offspring. Such weeding of the weak aids the herds, although you might not agree if you were the one weeded. Scientists have found wolf-killed moose with lungs so filled with tapeworm cysts it was amazing they could still breathe. During the early 1980s, pinkeye blinded scores of agile bighorn sheep in Yellowstone. Had wolves zeroed in on the sickly sheep, they might have halted the epidemic before it spread and sent sheep stumbling off cliffs.

The predators analyze their work. Mech watched wolves chase a moose and leave it bleeding. The wolves rested nearby, but every time the weary moose lay down, a wolf stepped forward and it rose. This happened over and over until the moose just couldn't keep it up.

When wolves reached Isle Royale across an unusual ice bridge, they winnowed marginal moose and the herd as a whole thrived. The number of moose bearing twins - a barometer of herd health - rose nearly seven times, to the highest rate ever documented in North America, probably because the survivors stood stronger and faced fewer rivals for food. Wolves may stabilize elk herds, like those in Yellowstone, that swing wildly from boom to bust, exhausting range grasses during mild years and dying by the thousands during hard winters. Through the ages, wolves left the stout elk, the fast deer, the fittest of any species to perpetuate their kind. That's why elk are stout and deer are fast today.

After the kill, blood stains the snow. Wolves lap it up. They crowd the carcass like kids surrounding an ice cream stand. They pull the insides out. Crunch. They crack the bones, gulp the marrow.

Gorged wolves laze, "meat drunk," as if they've just finished Thanksgiving dinner. Theirs is a feast-and-famine existence - days may pass without a kill. So wolves eat whatever they find, from moose to mice and anything in between, sometimes wolfing down food equal to one-fifth their body weight, the same as a 200-pound person eating 40 pounds at one sitting. If prey is vulnerable - weakened, perhaps, by drought or a hard winter - wolves may well kill more than they need, though they do the same before giving birth, stockpiling meat to feed yipping pups.

Just as wolves regulate their prey, though, their prey has a way of regulating them.

Wolf territories range from 30 to more than 1,000 square miles, swelling and contracting like balloons depending on how much room a pack needs to find meals. Well-fed packs need not range far. When food is scarce, though, or if they kill too much prey, territories bump up against each other and packs savagely defend their space. In such times of stress, alpha pairs may not bear pups. Two-year-old wolves typically scatter, looking to start their own packs; parents may boot them on their way if rations are tight.

Perhaps that was the lot of the one wolf Gerry snared. Two or three years old, the gray

People are not the only ones who enjoy hot springs. In winter, bison and other big game huddle in geyser basins, taking advantage of the natural warmth. LARRY MAYER

fledgling weighed 75 pounds when biologists showed up, pinned him to the snow with a modified pitchfork and collared him with a trusty radio transmitter. Released, the stunned wolf hesitated, then dashed away. Weeks later, beeps sent by the youngster's radio collar quickened, signaling that either the collar or its wearer was no longer moving.

When wildlife officers boarded their Skidoos and went looking for the Judas wolf, they found only blood and wisps of fur. The thick vinyl radio collar had been chewed like a dog's rawhide bone. Other wolves evidently had a notrespassing policy, strictly enforced.

As loyal, caring and social as wolves are with their own family, they are equally fierce in its defense.

As Gerry and I made our rounds, another trapper to the north snagged a tawny-gray wolf that soon donned a collar. Eight or nine months old, the female pup was already nearing the size of her mother, a big alpha as black as the shadows in nearby timber. Together, the mother and daughter would easily fare better than the trespassing wolf. A few months later, they would enter not another pack's territory, but an entirely new one.

Left: A whirlwind of controversy surrounds the historic federal project to repopulate Yellowstone Park with gray wolves, until now the one patch missing from the park's biological quilt.
ALAN AND SANDY CAREY

FOUR

"OPERATION WOLFSTOCK"

Beep. Beep. The tones came evenly, between 80 and 90 times a minute, echoing the heartbeat of the black female wolf lying on a table in the chilly garage of a provincial park in western Alberta, Canada. Beep. A mix of drugs stilled the creature as veterinarians and biologists checked her over like doctors tending a newborn. Beep. They opened her imposing jaw, gauging the keen canines with calipers. Beep. They spread the leathery pads on her feet, measuring five inches across. Hours before, the wolf been leading her pack over the coarse country between the McLeod and Embarras rivers. Now, this gang of humans drew blood from her front leg. They sprayed her for lice. They noticed blood under her tail, evidence the wolf was primed for breeding. They sifted the black-frosted-with-white fur on her belly, finding ample nipples, a sure sign she was the matriarch of her pack.

The alpha female.

"This is the best you could hope for," said L. David Mech, the biologist who had gotten his start watching wolves pull down moose at Isle Royale. He slipped his fingers down the wolf's lanky foreleg, as lengthy as a grown man's, aching to see this same limb pounding after moose, elk, anything. Pounding the rolling volcanic plateau that covers northwest Wyoming and is full of spraying geysers and what may be the most illustrious cross-stitch of wildlife in the continental United States. "She's good and healthy," said

Left: The U.S. government's dogged campaign against wolves thoroughly succeeded in exterminating them.
ALAN & SANDY CAREY

Mech, a bearded, balding federal researcher not prone to much elaboration. "Wouldn't she look good in Yellowstone?"

Mech's comment might have startled his predecessors, who foresaw a future without wolves. Now it was the other way around. "Operation Wolfstock," as the feds dubbed it, would send close to 150 wolves to their onetime home,

where they would hopefully take hold in coming years, assuring the future of their species.

From wear on the alpha's teeth, biologists figured she had been chomping the flesh and bone of prey for about four or five years, making her roughly middle age. A musky smell, like the aroma that pervades a pet store, rose from her coat. Under the pale glow of fluorescent lights,

Left: A helicopter carrying sharpshooters with tranquilizer guns hovers over a wolf running through the trees, lower right. LuRay Parker/WG&F/USFWS

Below: With assistance from Canadian veterinarian Beth Regehr, Yellowstone Park veterinarian Mark Johnson bolts a thick vinyl radio collar to a wolf captured in Canada. Such collars send out radio signals for roughly three years, aiding biologists trying to track wolf packs as they roam.
LuRay Parker/WG&F/USFWS

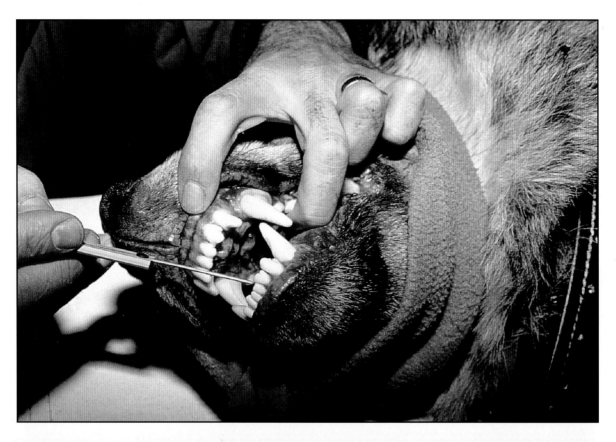

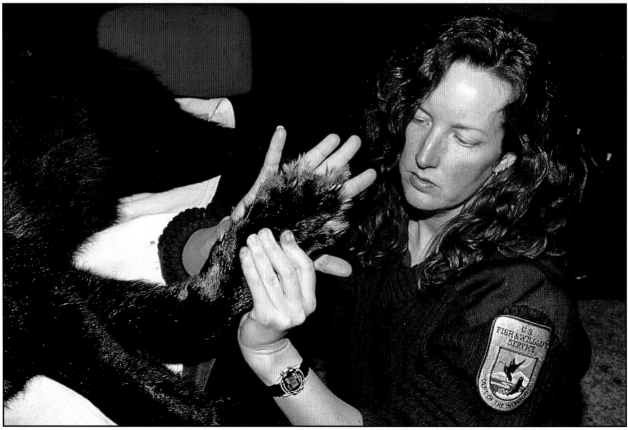

Above: Marksmen Ken Taylor and Mark McNay carry a drugged wolf to the steel crate that would hold it on its trip to Yellowstone Park.
LuRay Parker/WG&F/USFWS

Facing page
Top left: A wolf jaw is built to tear into prey and not let go. Biologists can estimate a wolf's age by the wear on its teeth.
LuRay Parker/WG&F/USFWS

Bottom: Biologists measured the dimensions of all wolves they captured. Alice Whitelaw, U.S. Fish and Wildlife Service, compares her palm to a wolf's.
LuRay Parker/WG&F/USFWS

the team snipped a tuft of hair and dropped it into a plastic bottle on a workbench, near a stack of radio collars. They rolled the wolf in a white canvas sling and hung it from a scale hooked on a broomstick. Three men hoisted the stick to their shoulders. It bowed toward the concrete floor, ready to snap. The needle said 98 pounds.

Across the garage, the alpha's tawny pup lay in a steel crate snug up against insulation blanketing the walls. Only 10 months old, the pup weighed 77 pounds, as much as a husky. She also wore a radio collar, thanks to her naive step, more than a month before, into a snare a trapper had rigged down toward the McLeod River, not far from the drainage of Wolf Creek. Her mother, the wolf on the examining table, now wore a collar, too. This pair of carnivores had long been nameless, faceless enigmas wandering the woodlands of Alberta, rarely showing themselves. Now the mother and daughter were about to ride the prow of a modern-day Noah's Ark south to the American West, where they would restake the claim of their long-lost ancestors.

Any wolf that U.S. teams could capture in Canada would go to Idaho, since wolves there would simply run wild into the corrugated backcountry in what biologists term a "hard release." For Yellowstone, the plan was trickier. Wolves would return via a "soft release." They would spend about two months inside one-acre pens of heavy chain-link fence, learning to like the country enough that they would not flee back to Canada. Wolves stuck in a pen with strangers will fight to defend their space, so biologists wanted related wolves, from the same pack, to stock each of three pens.

The alpha and her pup filled the bill.

It was a frigid December evening more than a month before when the amber pup had taken her first step toward Yellowstone by walking into

Left: Biologist Alice Whitelaw, USFWS, carries a wolf to a chilly garage in Canada where biologists and veterinarians will examine it and prepare it for shipment to the United States. LuRay Parker/WG&F/USFWS

Right: A sheepish wolf whiled away the hours before its trip from Canada to the United States lying quietly inside a small holding pen. LuRay Parker/WG&F/USFWS

the snare. That same bleak night, snares set by licensed trappers had strangled three fellows from her pack. But not the alpha. Somewhere out there in the sooty shadows, you can imagine the grand dame waiting, perhaps even watching, her eyes reflecting green, her nose lifted into the still air, her mind wondering about her kin. The next day, the brown-red-gray pup ran free with the new black radio collar binding her neck. Either she found her mother or her mother found her. They plodded on, accompanied by two other survivors from their pack. The pup grew up fast as the shrunken clan worked harder to pull down elk or moose for food. They had to kill. It's what they do.

Not far from the eventual destination of these wolves, friction over their future grew as forceful as their mighty jaws. Lawyers for the American Farm Bureau Federation dragged government biologists like Mech and Ed Bangs into a Casper, Wyoming, courtroom, aiming to show that the vicious ways of returning wolves would wreak havoc on local ranchers. Government agencies would shut down public lands to guard the wolves, the attorneys predicted. But a judge found "only fear and speculation of some livestock depredation in the indefinite future." Once again, the channel was clear.

Marksmen set out in helicopters over the timbered uplands - broken by river channels, lakes and meadows - following steady tones broadcast by some 15 wolves wearing miniature radio stations as necklaces. Depressed by the cold, fumes from pulp plants hung in hollows like soup in a bowl. Wolf fur blended with the terrain, but the sharpshooters knew where to look. The helicopters dipped, herding the slippery targets into logged gaps for a clear shot. The wolves ran, dodging and turning like a marble on a tilted table. The copters dropped, putting the muzzle of a big-barrelled shotgun no more than 20 feet from the racing wolves, and, WHAP, tranquilizer darts stabbed their hides. For the bewildered wolves, this probably spun the scene into further

disarray. The huge pinwheel in the sky was enough without this spike jabbing into my backside like some kind of metal mosquito and now .. the .. trees .. are ... hazy ... the ... ground .... is .... rolling .... and ..... rising ..... and ..... slamming ...... into ...... my .... face.

When the sharpshooters gave chase, they took down the tawny pup and her mother, too. A biologist shelved the duo on the front seat of his pickup and drove them to the metal-sided garage, where they gave up their weights and dimensions and had plastic tags clamped to their ears. Wolves headed for Yellowstone wore red tags. Those destined for Idaho bore blue. Yellow went, temporarily, to those with an undetermined destination. Tags on the alpha labeled her red-9; her daughter became red-7.

As wolves, some in bunches, some alone, fell to the finger-sized tranquilizer darts, biologists plotted strategy like coaches devising plays for a big game. Marking the capture of each wolf on a map, they judged whether to send helicopters after more wolves from a certain pack, even if it meant tracking them through thick timber, or search out entirely new packs. Weather was a factor, along with time (daylight lasted only eight hours at this latitude), money (helicopters run $500 or more per hour), biology (breeding season was approaching and wolves needed to be in place by then) and politics (more legal maneuvers were in the offing).

Left: Sharpshooter Ken Taylor sits behind a wolf he had just hit with a tranquilizer dart while flying above the running animal in a helicopter. LuRay Parker/WG&F/USFWS

*A horse trailer serves as the carriage that
hauled the first wolves through Yellowstone
Park's entrance arch in January 1995.*
BOB ZELLAR

"I feel like I'm in the eye of a hurricane," said Steven Fritts, the main wolf capture strategist. He was standing in the garage that had become wolf central. Fritts is a soft-spoken federal biologist with the U. S. Fish and Wildlfe Service who began his career pursuing wolves that bothered livestock in Minnesota. Snow fell outside. It looked as if Fritts might rather be out there, with the wolves. "It's hard to remember everything I need to worry about," he said. "Dealing with the wolves is probably the easiest part."

Wolves that realize they have been had, by a snare or whatever, resign themselves to the consequences. Throw a net over them and they cower. They are used to a strict pack hierarchy where insubordination can mean death. A couple of biologists toted the tawny pup from the examining table on an Army-green stretcher and manhandled her into a holding pen the size of a minivan. Her head bobbed like a drunkard's as she struggled, in her drugged stupor, to see what the heck was going on.

"That's what you look like after a Saturday night binge," offered Joe Fontaine, another U. S. biologist, who was throwing more straw into the pen for a wolf bed.

With full stretchers, clattering helicopters and ringing phones, the place had the feel of a M*A*S*H unit.

In the garage, veterinarians worked over another wolf. They had consulted vets at the San Diego Zoo to learn how best to examine U.S.-bound wolves for injuries or disease. Drugs sedated the animals during exams, while blindfolds shielded them from human commotion should the tranquilizers wear thin. Doses of penicillin warded off stress-related infections and tiny hunks of wolf flesh went toward DNA studies. Vets also pinched each animal's tongue with a plastic clip, wired to a digital device that tracked

Above: U.S. Interior Secretary Bruce Babbitt lent a hand by carrying crated wolves to their pens in Yellowstone Park. Decades earlier, his ranching family had backed the elimination of wolves from the West. BOB ZELLAR

Left: Wildlife experts had to prod some wolves before they would leave the safe seclusion of their shipping crates. But the wolves in Idaho did not always seem eager to be prodded. LURAY PARKER/WG&F/USFWS

the wolf's pulse and the oxygen content of its blood. One wolf had died when a tranquilizer dart pierced its lungs. When another wolf was on the examining table, the amount of oxygen in its blood plummeted. A lung had collapsed. The vets pulled out an artificial breathing apparatus - just as doctors would in an emergency room - and blew air down its throat. They found that a dart had punctured the lung. They sutured the tear. The wolf ended up in Yellowstone.

For all the years that had led up to it, the wolves made the trip from Canada rather quickly. One at a time they got shoved into steel shipping containers with the warning: "U.S. Government - For Official Use Only." A U-Haul truck ("America's Moving Adventure") carted the crates to a U.S. Forest Service cargo plane, which flew south to Montana. Their crates strapped to the floor, the engines droning, Canadian prairies and the American border sliding beneath them, the

wolves hardly moved. They were probably scared. Wolves survive by fleeing or deferring when something bigger menaces. This time, they could not flee, so they hunkered down.

Darkness had swallowed the Lamar Valley in Yellowstone about the time the plane landed, still many miles away. Three fenced pens lay quiet, holding only the meat of elk and deer hit by automobiles. Two Native Americans climbed up onto a car-sized sled that, powered by a pair of mules, would soon slide the crated wolves up easy grades to the pens. Recalling his Sioux and Crow ancestry, Scott Frazier spread a buffalo robe and burned a braid of cedar. Spears of moonlight struck the snow. John Potter sang, welcoming the creature who had long been a model to his Ojibway tribe - a model of how to live, how to look out for family and how to hunt.

"The wolf broke new trails for us, leading us to new ground," he said, his voice amplified

Above: A mule-drawn sled hauls shipping crates containing wolves toward a one-acre pen in Yellowstone Park's Lamar Valley.
BOB ZELLAR

by the vast quiet but overwhelmed by the outstretched valley and volcanic ridges that pointed at the stars. "Here tonight, we've had the opportunity to return the favor."

With the ceremony done, the wolves pulled closer. Some 4,000 wolves live in Alberta, so the first dozen that went south to America, with nearly 100 more to follow in the next five years, would not be missed. But if their departure made little difference in Canada, it made all the difference in the United States.

National Park Service patrol cars led the way under Yellowstone National Park's entrance arch at midmorning, a dozen days into 1995. A horse trailer followed. The steel crates inside were hidden from locals, schoolchildren and reporters who lined either side of the road. Applause and human howls pierced the cold. The wolves were probably not in any mood to howl.

Clumps of snowflakes burst atop the steel crates as the sled hauled them to a pen up Crystal Creek. The alpha female with the green eyes

and her tawny pup rode another sled to a pen tucked along Rose Creek. They smelled meat left for them as their first taste of Yellowstone.

If this story were simple, it ought to end there. But you know by now it's not. Many local folks, even if they had railed against wolves and the feds who would bring them back, had more or less resigned themselves to dealing with the cutthroat carnivores. But they were not happy about it.

"We lost the battle," Stan Flitner said the night before the wolves arrived. He grazes his cattle on the sagebrush steppes of northwest Wyoming about 150 miles from Yellowstone's boundary. "It seems to be the law of the land that we've got to reintroduce an animal that's going to cause nothing but problems." That same night, the Farm Bureau had taken its legal fight one step further, to a federal appeals court, which issued a stay insisting no new wolves roam Yellowstone or Idaho.

So the wolves remained in their steel crates, breathing the air of their new roosts. Wolves on their way to Idaho waited in an airplane hangar as Nez Perce Indians offered prayers. The Idaho wolves had special fans: classrooms of children who had chosen names for them and colored and inscribed the radio collars each wolf would wear. One bore the name Chat Chaht: in Nez Perce, "older brother."

As twilight cloaked the Lamar again, the wolves gazing at their new domain from steel boxes, licking at ice for water, the place seemed an eternity from a courtroom in Denver, where a signed paper and a phone call sent Yellowstone National Park biologists Mike Phillips and Wayne Brewster moving toward the pens. Phillips was a bit preoccupied by the thought of his son Samuel, born the day before. Both had dealt with wolves, but they knew this was different. They slogged through snow, tracing the trail

left by the sled earlier in the day and, at the first pen, lifted metal panels blocking the ends of the crates and left.

Within a day of freedom for the Yellowstone wolves, the first four wolves ran loose in Idaho. They stepped forward, peeking at onlookers from their boxes and then bolted, streaks of gray darting this way and that, around the trees and gone.

As Brewster and Phillips hiked toward the Rose Creek pen, where they had left the alpha and her pup, the overcast sky shattered into clouds. Creamy light bounced off the moon and tinted the clouds silver - an Ansel Adams sky.

Brewster turned to Phillips and said, "You know, nobody will ever do this again."

They had oriented the crates against the fence, so exiting wolves would brush the chain link and know better than to race across their pen and smack into the same fence. The biologists slid the ends open and glanced in. The alpha was curled up in the back, shying from the humans. But the tawny pup was sitting on her haunches, gawking right back at them.

The pair of biologists strode out of the pen, ready to leave the wolves alone for the first time in days. As they did, they heard a clink: the pup swiping the fence. They turned to look; there she was, blazing through snow like a bird through the air.

The wolf was back.

Left: Gray wolves returning to Yellowstone Park and central Idaho must escape the antipathy that, decades ago, drove them to extinction in the American West.
ALAN & SANDY CAREY

Right: Nez Perce Indians Horace Axtell and Allen V. Pinkhan Sr. bless gray wolves headed for central Idaho during a layover at the Missoula, Montana, airport. Indian tribes celebrated the return of a missing biological link in the West.
LURAY PARKER/WG&F/USFWS

ENTER THE WOLF

Looking through binoculars at a ridge across the Lamar Valley, Bob Crabtree raised his palm, demanding silence. The scaled trunk of a fir wound between boulders as big as trucks and spread above our heads into bristling branches that deflected the midwinter sun. Droppings about our feet charted the travels of elk that had passed before. But our eyes were aimed at a wooded nook among boxy boulders across the Lamar.

From hills to the east, toward the square gulch that funnels the Lamar River, came a sharp whine, not quite a bark and not quite a howl, but a rough merger of the two. It started on a high note and tapered into silence.

"Did you hear that?" asked Crabtree, an ecologist who had been studying the wildlife of Yellowstone Park's northern range for more than five years. "That was definitely longer than normal."

Wolves had indeed arrived. One pack was pacing its pen, out of sight in the nook across the valley, casing the chain-link for a window to freedom. But it was not the wolves we were hearing. It was coyotes, and they were noisier than usual. The echo of one of their ensemble yelps had hardly dissolved into the snow-swept Lamar before they belted out a new one. We watched one coyote through a spotting scope: it swerved along the ridge, looking down toward the wolf pen, perplexed by the odd, new neighbors.

Left: Returning wolves to Yellowstone and central Idaho will test the strength of the Endangered Species Act. Critics complain the law favors wildlife over local economies.
ALAN & SANDY CAREY

Above: Bob Crabtree has been studying the wildlife of Yellowstone Park's northern range for more than five years. MICHAEL MILSTEIN

Coyotes and wolves howl, as songbirds chirp, to tell others: Hey, this is our spot. But these coyotes had inherited their post as Yellowstone's top dog. When they yelled their warnings, we wondered whether they knew who was listening.

For a new master hunter had scaled the biological pyramid. The baffled coyotes eyeing the pens, the ravens circling in a pulsing fog above, the bison bulldozing snow with their skulls, the elk lazing in the sun and all the rest would soon have to make way, just as humans would, for a new kingpin.

Reams of research paved the long road wolves had followed to the American West. Stacked one atop the other, the studies would outreach Old Faithful. But when wolves finally alighted on local soil, all the crystal-ball forecasts slipped into the same file as snapshots of the world's best-known geyser: interesting as a reference, but always surpassed by the real thing.

Never before had people resurrected a top carnivore they had relentlessly erased from the map. By bringing wolves back to Yellowstone and Idaho, Americans had commenced a great natural experiment, one that would prove not only how critical wolves are to the intricate ecology of the Rockies, but also how vital they are to our own outlook on the world of all things wild. Wolves are not a cure-all for every environmental fault. But the predators will no doubt send shudders radiating through the web of life like

Right: Feeble buffalo calves may be vulnerable to wolves, but decades ago on the Great Plains, big, lumbering bison learned that by surrounding their young like a living fortress, they could keep wolves away.
Bob Zellar

Below: Coyotes will lose their place at the top of the food chain, and may decline in number, when wolves begin hunting on same ground. Larry Mayer

ripples in a pond when a pebble falls in. Stand next to a belching hot water cauldron in one of Yellowstone's surreal geyser basins and you feel the same sort of quivers beneath your feet. Wolves are now the epicenter.

"Nobody's ever been able to watch this before," offered Crabtree, his eyes still peeled toward the other side of the Lamar.

Biological tremors may first strike coyotes, diminutive versions of wolves that compete with their outsized cousins and had multiplied while wolves were gone. But there is not room at the top for everyone. Mightier wolves ought to knock coyotes back down the ladder and take over their ground, though in lesser numbers. Because wolves devour more meat than coyotes, they will hone their jaws mainly on hulking elk and bison, easing life for rare trumpeter swans and other coyote staples, perhaps even domestic sheep on public lands neighboring Yellowstone.

With coyotes in check, a slot may open for the next canine echelon, the fox. Early trappers and explorers reported lots of red, bushy-tailed foxes. But when wolves disappeared, foxes dropped off, too, probably because coyotes would not put up with such a close rival.

Keep following the waves. Fewer coyotes means an easier time for such small meat-eaters

Above: Mike Phillips is Yellowstone's top wolf biologist. He recently presided over the return of the red wolf to coastal North Carolina, the only previous wolf restoration effort.
DAVID GRUBBS

Top left: Wildlife, from moose to marmots like the one here, must make way as gray wolves send biological shock waves rippling across the Yellowstone landscape.
LARRY MAYER

Preceding page: While wolves completed Yellowstone Park's assembly of wildlife, not everyone was pleased. The unyielding Montana Legislature urged federal wildlife managers to also introduce wolves in Washington, D.C., San Francisco and New York City's Central Park.
LARRY MAYER

Above: Wolves are stealthy hunters, relying on their keen eyes and noses to detect prey and on teamwork to bring it down. Native American hunting strategies reflected the cunning of wolves. ALAN & SANDY CAREY

Right: Even colorful song birds may benefit from the return of gray wolves to Yellowstone, by feeding on insects drawn to carcasses killed by wolves. BOB ZELLAR

Right: The black alpha female that had come from the McLeod River country of Alberta, Canada, with her tawny pup, looks out of her pen in Yellowstone Park, awaiting liberty.
YELLOWSTONE NATIONAL PARK

Facing page: With wolves back in the neighborhood, elk may grow more wary as they seek meals, to avoid becoming meals. BOB ZELLAR

as badgers, weasels and eagles. If they cull the teeming thousands of mice and voles, there will be fewer rodents to nibble grass down to a nub. Tracts burned by the epic fires of 1988 will dissolve into meadows. That leaves prime greenery for elk, bison, deer and antelope - which provides more meat for wolves.

Like the green-eyed alpha and tawny pup. When a second batch of wolves arrived in Yellowstone a week after they had, the mother-daughter pair got a partner: a stately, 122-pound male wolf with a beefy body nearly as long (his tail included) as a professional basketball player is tall. He was light-gray and, considering his size and maturity, had been the alpha male of his pack in Canada. Another wolf from the pack went to Idaho; the rest had escaped the helicopter and darts.

So matchmaking biologists molded a new pack, something nobody had done before. As the gray male rose from his crate, the alpha female stood against the far fence, a black silhouette within a canopy of trees, her ears cocked, staring at him. He grabbed a couple of mouthfuls of snow to quench his thirst and waded into the smooth powder. When the two adults met, they postured in the standoffish way of a new and uneasy couple, until he nipped at her and swung his head atop her shoulders, declaring his dominance. She would have none of it, and whirled around, snapping at him. He backed off. All this in a matter of a few minutes. From then on, the two connected in a kind of romantic equilibrium and bedded down on spongy pine needles together. When he would saunter by, she would flip her tail to the side, the wolfish equivalent of hiking her skirt.

"What we were seeing is really what you could call flirting," said Mike Phillips as the tires of his government pickup splashed through slush

on the road to the Lamar. We were talking about mixing the two alphas and the tawny pup - known as red 7, 9 and 10. Phillips, Yellowstone's top wolf biologist, who had just before presided over the return of endangered red wolves to coastal North Carolina (the only previous large-scale wolf restoration effort), was explaining why he prefers numbers to names. There's a practical reason: people who follow one wolf might be crestfallen if good old Freddie gets hit by a truck or dies an unglamorous death - as one red wolf had - by choking on a raccoon kidney. There is also a bigger reason: we should value wolves on their own terms, without names that would make them fit into ours.

"The world is vastly different through the eyes of a wolf than through the eyes of a human and we have to respect that," said Phillips, his voice charged with evangelistic enthusiasm. "They're not here to be pets. They're here because

it's the right thing to do."

His reasoning made sense, but it seemed the wolves deserved more than numbers. They were individuals: red-7, the bold pup; red-10, the haughty alpha male (vets called him "the big guy") who might ignore others and watch a chickadee, as if to say, I know you're there and I don't care; and red-13, an elderly slate-blue wolf picked on by the rest of his pack. Numbers seemed too dry for these beings we had run through such a gauntlet on their way to the West. We had wiped them out and now we wanted them back. In truth, the wolves had returned on our terms, not theirs.

One warm winter day with the first wolves still in holding, Phillips and I scrambled up a shaded, icy hill to peer into one of the circular one-acre pens. Sunlight glittered off distant snow like a million flickering Christmas lights. Soon the wolves would hunt, eat and drink in this view. Spindly skeletons of aspen cast zebra stripes on the snow. Phillips stands short and stocky with a baseball build (his father played briefly for the Philadelphia Phillies). He scaled the slippery slope like a mountain goat.

There they were.

A hundred yards below, flowing back and forth, back and forth, tracing a dirty trail along the 10-foot fence. They no doubt wanted out. A few had cut their jowls when restlessly tugging at the chain-link. Their gait was like no other, an exaggerated lope that reminded me of the floppy legs of a marionette. Ravens squawked. The alpha male stood out. He carried himself higher, his tail rigid, extending his five-foot backbone like a switchblade. It's what dogs do when defending their backyard. All the rest drooped their tails toward the snow.

As other biologists dragged hunks of elk into the pen, the wolves hugged the wall, as far from the people as they could get. They had survived in Canada only because they avoided humans. Plans called for shipping about 15 wolves each to Yellowstone and central Idaho for three to five years. Ten breeding packs, or about 100 wolves altogether, must populate each spot before federal agencies rule the species recovered and let the states manage wolves outside the national park. Federal plans forecast such thriving numbers by 2002. As their roots grow deeper and they realize they are protected in Yellowstone and nearby Grand Teton National Park, wolves will show themselves, most often in open flats and valleys where prey is plentiful. In Denali National Park in Alaska, about 15 percent of visitors see wolves. What people will not find is danger: there are no reliable records of healthy, wild wolves injuring people. Bees, meanwhile, kill upwards of 40 people each year.

Road-killed carcasses that assured each of the penned wolves 15 pounds of meat every day fattened them up. The alphas got into the spirit of the mating season - the month or so centered around Valentine's Day - and paired up, though their coupling did not guarantee pups come spring. In time, they howled, responding to coyotes with a guttural admonition of their own. Again, I wondered, could the coyotes realize who they were dealing with?

Probably the buffalo placidly rummaging for shoots in snowdrifts just outside the pen did not. They cast bored glances at the jagged-jawed creatures inside. During bitter winters, hundreds of buffalo that exit Yellowstone are gunned down because of fear that they carry disease that could infect cattle. So many thousands of bison jam Yellowstone that an electric fence surrounded the pens, not to keep the wolves in, but to keep the bison from smashing through on their grass-seeking strolls.

From their side of the fence, the pacing wolves eyed the bison. A recovered wolf population may kill around 1,200 prey animals each year and will, without a doubt, trim the nearly 100,000 buffalo, elk, deer and moose in and around Yellowstone. Computer models predict the 40,000 elk could decline as much as 30 percent in the extreme and other species at lesser rates. While wolves may steal trophies from hunters, though, they will not wipe out all of their prey. It was people, not wolves, who eliminated the buffalo, which had long flourished, with wolves, on the Great Plains. Bison called on teamwork to defeat the predators: adults enclosed young in wolf-tight circles that left worn rings on the prairie.

The buffalo had ambled on by the time Phillips and others opened the first pen on an overcast March night. Staring freedom in the face, the wolves retreated, shying from the gate where their feeders had come and gone. Biologists had to snip a hole in the fence, as if they

Above: While waiting for their release, wolves paced their circular pens. The pens were round so there would be no corners where wolves could climb out. BOB ZELLAR

were busting cohorts out of prison, before a few wolves finally dashed out. But the hulking alpha male that had joined the female and her tawny pup never hesitated. When biologists climbed toward his pen to cut a new gap in the fence, they met him, 300 yards away, on their side of the fence. He howled a deep howl, perhaps a signal to the female and pup he had come to think of as his pack. A small herd of bison paid him no mind. But the biologists backed off, giving the chieftain room to roam, to join the buffalo, elk and coyotes and to spill his first blood on the melting spring snow.

And the biological tremors roll on. Wolves may be nimble hunters, but grizzly bears are bigger and may commandeer wolf kills for themselves. Golden eagles and black-and-white magpies could get leftovers. Foxes, too - a payback for the many times wolves renovate fox dens into their own. Decomposing carcasses yanked down by wolves feed bugs that feed birds like the orange-yellow Western tanager, which might fly south for the winter in greater numbers, brightening the jungles of Central America. Mountain lions can kill more animals than wolves, but wolves may usurp lion kills. Elk on alert for wolves may troop out of fragile streambeds, letting willows and other wetland plants flourish, creating shelter for more songbirds. That, in turn, may draw beavers to engineer dams to create new ponds to hold more trout to bend the poles of more human anglers.

And the shock waves will inevitably rattle ranchers. Wolves will leave the national park and kill livestock. In 1905, a cattleman in the steep Sunlight Basin of northwest Wyoming told of guarding his herd from wolves for seven weeks running and added, "Yellowstone National Park was the breeding ground, or at least the refuge, for these predatory beasts."

To smooth the way for wolves this time, the environmental group Defenders of Wildlife has pledged to pay ranchers for wolf-killed livestock, as it has in northern Montana. Federal authorities have promised to deal quickly with wolves that raid herds and not lock up public lands for the wolf's benefit. Wild wolves have not ruined ranchers elsewhere and government predictions suggest their annual toll would run less than one-tenth of one percent of the more than 400,000 livestock near Yellowstone. But for many, the predators remain a bitter pill that will sound out the integrity of the Endangered Species Act, a law that has saved the alligator and bald eagle but failed others and driven a wedge between the economy and the environment. Even while the first packs prowled their pens, the Wyoming Legislature, in a dominance display of its own, offered a $1,000 bounty on any wolf roaming beyond Yellowstone's borders. The governor vetoed it.

Anyone can work the numbers. Tourists eager to see wolves and hear them join Nature's chorus may dump millions more dollars into the economy; hunters displaced by wolves may take dollars elsewhere. Returning the wolf to the West will cost around $13 million. In the end, dollars are fleeting. What's not is the size of our world and our place in it.

And whether we can leave a place for wolves.

If there is such a place, it ought to be Yellowstone, the largest intact ecosystem in the Lower 48. On a brilliant day, Mike Phillips and I crunched through snow onto a rise north of Specimen Ridge. As we talked, he chucked hunks of ice, like frozen baseballs, out toward Hellroaring Creek, toward the jumbled crags where wolf pups had wobbled so many decades ago. Not far up the Lamar was Soda Butte, where the last wolves had died. As much as he wants to judge wolves on their terms, Phillips could not help but cast this in human dimensions. That is, after all, what we understand. If we could hand the wolves - black alpha, tawny pup, any wolf - glossy travel brochures full of pretty wildlife shots, they'd opt for the all-expenses-paid trip to Yellowstone and its banquet on the hoof.

But we cannot. To undo the past, we're charting new ground, testing our own fortitude as much as that of the wolves. Somewhere out there in the sunny valley, edged by lodgepole pines, were the black and gray alphas and the

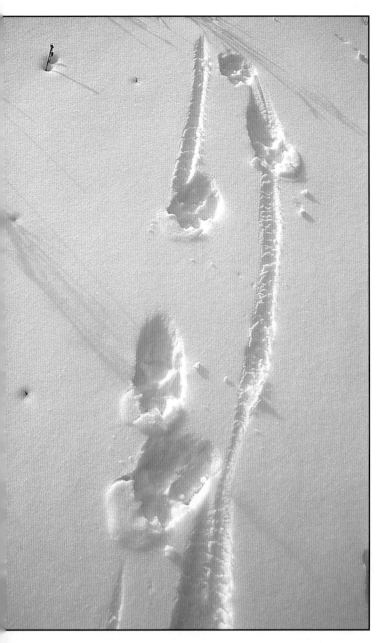

tawny pup, a vanguard that may lead wolves back to other slices of the wilds: Colorado, the desert Southwest, the Northeast forests. Only they and their descendants know if they will go along. Some may leave. Some may die. Mike Phillips wants the wolf project known for - he has the speech down pat - "rigorous thinking" and "open-mindedness." But he does not have all the answers. And he gladly admits it.

He already looks forward to the day, years from now, when the questions run out, when the biologists can turn off the electronic gadgetry that points them toward the radio collars all the wolves wear. When they can, for that matter, let the wolves shed the collars we all have placed on them.

"I look forward to the day we leave the buggers alone," he says.

Surely they do, too.

Above: After their release in late March, 1995, wild wolves left their tracks in Yellowstone Park for the first time in close to seven decades. Biologists will monitor the wolves for years to learn how they behave in a new environment.
ALAN & SANDY CAREY

Overleaf: A federal environmental impact statement as thick as a metropolitan telephone book predicted wolves would cull, but not destroy, game herds in Yellowstone Park and central Idaho.
LARRY MAYER

The confluence of the Snake and the Heart rivers in Yellowston Park. LARRY MAYER

BIBLIOGRAPHY

Barker, Rocky. *Saving All the Parts: Reconciling Economics and the Endangered Species Act.* Washington, D.C.: Island Press, 1993.

Bartlett, Richard A. *Yellowstone: A Wilderness Besieged.* Tucson, Ariz.: The University of Arizona Press, 1985.

Bass, Rick. *The Ninemile Wolves.* Livingston, Mont.: Clark City Press, 1992.

Bennett, Larry E. *Colorado Gray Wolf Recovery: A Biological Feasibility Study.* Denver: U.S. Fish and Wildlife Service in cooperation with University of Wyoming Fish and Wildlife Cooperative Research Unit, 1994.

Chase, Alston. *Playing God in Yellowstone.* San Diego: Harcourt Brace Jovanovich, 1987.

Clary, David A. *The Place Where Hell Bubbled Up: A History of the First National Park.* Moose, Wyo.: Homestead Publishing, 1993.

Despain, Don G. *Yellowstone Vegetation.* Boulder, Colo.: Roberts Rinehart Publishers, 1990.

Haines, Aubrey L. *The Yellowstone Story, Vols. 1-2.* Yellowstone National Park: Yellowstone Library and Museum Association, 1977.

Jones, William A. *Report Upon the Reconnaissance of Northwestern Wyoming Made in the Summer of 1873.* Washington: U.S. Government Printing Office, 1874.

Langford, Nathaniel Pitt. *The Discovery of Yellowstone Park.* Lincoln, Neb.: University of Nebraska Press, 1972.

Lawrence, R.D. *In Praise of Wolves.* New York: Henry Holt and Company, 1986.

Leopold, Aldo. *A Sand County Almanac.* New York: Oxford University Press, 1949.

Link, Mike, and Kate Crowley. *Following the Pack: The World of Wolf Research.* Stillwater, Minn.: Voyageur Press, 1994.

Lopez, Barry Holstun. *Of Wolves and Men.* New York: Charles Scribner's Sons, 1978.

Mader. T.R. W*olf Reintroduction in the Yellowstone National Park: A Historical Perspective.* Gillette, Wyo.: Common Man Institute, 1988.

Matthiessen, Peter. *Wildlife In America.* New York: Viking Penguin Inc., 1987.

McIntyre, Rick. *A Society of Wolves: National Parks and the Battle Over the Wolf.* Stillwater, Minn.: Voyageur Press, 1993.

Mech, L. David. *The Way of the Wolf.* Stillwater, Minn.: Voyageur Press, 1991.

Mech, L. David. *The Wolf: The Ecology and Behavior of an Endangered Species.* Garden City, New York: The Natural History Press, 1970.

Murie, Adolph. *A Naturalist in Alaska.* New York: The Devin-Adair Company, 1961.

Murie, Adolph. *Ecology of the Coyote in the Yellowstone.* Washington, D.C.: U.S. Government Printing Office, 1940.

Murie, Adolph. *The Wolves of Mount McKinley.* Seattle: University of Washington Press, 1944.

Russell, Osborne. *Journal of a Trapper.* Lincoln, Neb.: University of Nebraska Press, 1986.

Savage, Candace. *Wolves.* San Francisco: Sierra Club Books, 1988.

Schullery, Paul. *The Bears of Yellowstone.* Yellowstone National Park: Yellowstone Library and Museum Association, 1980.

Samson, John G., ed. *The Worlds of Ernest Thompson Seton.* New York: Alfred A. Knopf, 1976.

Seton, Ernest Thompson. *Wild Animals I Have Known.* New York: Charles Scribner's Sons, 1911.

U.S. Fish and Wildlife Service. *Northern Rocky Mountain Wolf Recovery Plan.* Denver: U.S. Fish and Wildlife Service, 1987.

U.S. Fish and Wildlife Service. *Final Environmental Impact Statement: The Reintroduction of Gray Wolves to Yellowstone National Park and Central Idaho.* Helena, Mont.: U.S. Fish and Wildlife Service, 1994.

Varley, J.D., and W.G. Brewster, eds. *Wolves For Yellowstone? A Report to the United States Congress, vols. 1-4.* Yellowstone National Park: National Park Service, 1990, 1992.

Weaver, John. *The Wolves of Yellowstone: History, Ecology and Status.* Yellowstone National Park: National Park Service, 1978.

Whittlesey, Lee H. *Yellowstone Place Names.* Helena, Mont.: Montana Historical Society Press, 1988.

Young, Stanley Paul. *The Wolf in North American History.* Caldwell, Idaho: The Caxton Printers, Ltd., 1946.

Young, Stanley Paul. *The Wolves of North America.* New York: Dover Publications, Inc., 1944.

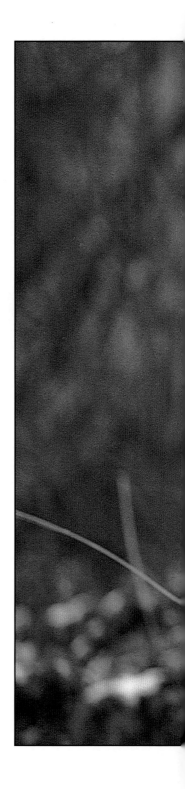

For people, the mournful howl of the wolf echoes the essence of wild lands. For wolves, the howl broadcasts practical messages to other wolves within earshot. ALAN & SANDY CAREY

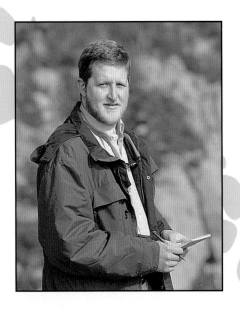

Michael Milstein began covering Wyoming, including Yellowstone National Park, for The Billings Gazette in 1989. He and his wife, Sue, live in Cody, Wyoming. His stories on Yellowstone have won first place awards from the Montana Newspaper Association for outdoor, investigative and in-depth reporting, as well as awards from the Society of Professional Journalists. In 1994, he received the Ray Bruner Science Writing Award for articles on the microbes of Yellowstone hot springs. Both the Greater Yellowstone Coalition and the Wyoming Wildlife Federation have recognized him as environmental writer of the year.

A 1988 graduate of Duke University, Milstein worked as an intern at the Los Angeles Times, The Sacramento Bee and The News and Observer in Raleigh, North Carolina. His work has appeared in those publications, as well as Reader's Digest, Outside, Science, National Parks, The San Diego Union-Tribune, The Boston Globe, The Christian Science Monitor and High Country News. In 1993, he completed a six-week science writing fellowship at the Marine Biological Laboratory in Woods Hole, Massachusetts.